Second-Grade Math Minutes

One Hundred Minutes to Better Basic Skills

Written by

Angela Higgs

Editor
Marsha Elyn Wright

Illustrator
Corbin Hillam

Cover Illustrator
Rick Grayson

Designers
Moonhee Pak and Mary L. Gagné

Cover Designer
Barbara Peterson

Art Director
Tom Cochrane

Project Director
Carolea Williams

© 2002 Creative Teaching Press, Inc., Huntington Beach, CA 92649
Reproduction of activities in any manner for use in the classroom and not for commercial sale is permissible.
Reproduction of these materials for an entire school or for a school system is strictly prohibited.

Table of Contents

Introduction

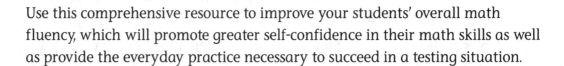

The focus of *Second-Grade Math Minutes* is math fluency—teaching students to solve problems effortlessly and rapidly. The problems in this book provide students with practice in key areas of second-grade math instruction, including

- using a number line
- skip counting
- basic addition and subtraction
- story problems
- graphs
- writing numbers
- plane and space figures
- money
- measurement
- perimeter
- fractions

Use this comprehensive resource to improve your students' overall math fluency, which will promote greater self-confidence in their math skills as well as provide the everyday practice necessary to succeed in a testing situation.

Second-Grade Math Minutes features 100 "Minutes." Each Minute consists of ten classroom-tested problems for students to try to complete in one minute. Because each Minute includes questions of varying degrees of difficulty, the amount of time students need to complete each Minute will vary at first. This unique format offers students an ongoing opportunity to improve their own fluency in a manageable, nonthreatening format. The quick, one-minute format combined with instant feedback makes this a challenging and motivational assignment students will look forward to each day. Students become active learners as they discover mathematical relationships and apply acquired understanding to the solution of realistic problems in each Minute.

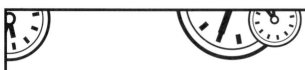

How to Use This Book

Second-Grade Math Minutes is designed to be implemented in numerical order. Students who need the most support will find the order of skills as introduced most helpful in building and retaining confidence and success. For example, the first time that students are asked to solve a word problem, an illustration is provided. Eventually, students are asked to solve word problems without the support of an illustration.

Second-Grade Math Minutes can be used in a variety of ways. Use one Minute a day for warm-up activities, bell-work, review, assessment, or a homework assignment. Keep in mind that students will get the most benefit from their daily Minute if they receive immediate feedback. If you assign the Minute as homework, correct it in class at the beginning of the day.

If you use the Minutes as a timed activity, place the paper facedown on the students' desks, or display it as a transparency. Use a clock or kitchen timer to measure one minute. Encourage students to concentrate on completing each problem successfully and not to dwell on problems they cannot complete. At the end of the minute, have students stop working. Then, read the answers from the answer key (pages 108–112), or display them on a transparency. Have students correct their own work and record their score on the Minute Journal reproducible (page 6). Then, have the class go over each problem together to discuss the solution(s). Spend more time on problems that were clearly challenging for most of the class. Tell students that difficult problems will appear on future Minutes and they will have other opportunities for success.

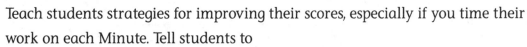

Teach students strategies for improving their scores, especially if you time their work on each Minute. Tell students to

- leave more time-consuming problems for last
- come back to problems they are unsure of after they have completed all other problems
- make educated guesses when they encounter problems they are unfamiliar with
- rewrite word problems as number problems
- use mental math wherever possible

Students will learn to apply these strategies to other timed-test situations.

The Minutes are designed to improve math fluency and should not be included as part of a student's overall math grade. However, the Minutes provide an excellent opportunity for you to see which skills the class as a whole needs to practice or review. This knowledge will help you plan the content of future math lessons. A class that consistently has difficulty with reading graphs, for example, may make excellent use of your lesson in that area, especially if they know they will have other opportunities to achieve success in this area on future Minutes. Have students file their Math Journal and Minutes for that week in a location accessible to you both. Class discussions of the problems will help you identify which math skills to review. However, you may find it useful to review the Minutes on a weekly basis before sending them home with students at the end of the week.

While you will not include student Minute scores in your formal grading, you may wish to recognize improvements by awarding additional privileges or offering a reward if the entire class scores above a certain level for a week or more. Showing students that you recognize their efforts provides additional motivation to succeed!

Minute Journal

Name _____

Minute	Date	Score	Minute	Date	Score	Minute	Date	Score	Minute	Date	Score
1			26			51			76		
2			27			52			77		
3			28			53			78		
4			29			54			79		
5			30			55			80		
6			31			56			81		
7			32			57			82		
8			33			58			83		
9			34			59			84		
10			35			60			85		
11			36			61			86		
12			37			62			87		
13			38			63			88		
14			39			64			89		
15			40			65			90		
16			41			66			91		
17			42			67			92		
18			43			68			93		
19			44			69			94		
20			45			70			95		
21			46			71			96		
22			47			72			97		
23			48			73			98		
24			49			74			99		
25			50			75			100		

Second-Grade Math Minutes © 2002 Creative Teaching Press

Scope and Sequence

· ·

Minute 1

Name _____

1. Write the missing number. _____

2. How many apples in all? _____ apples

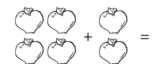

3. Kevin's mom has 6 cookies. She gave 2 cookies to Kevin. How many cookies are left? _____ cookies

For questions 4 and 5, count. Write the number.

4. _____

5. _____

6. Use <, >, or, =.   6 ____ 3

Use the number line to complete questions 7 and 8.

7. $6 + 2 =$ _____

8. $10 - 7 =$ _____

For questions 9 and 10, circle the name of the shape.

9. ☐   triangle   circle   square

10. ▽   triangle   circle   square

Second-Grade Math Minutes © 2002 Creative Teaching Press

Minute 2

Name _____

For questions 1 and 2, use <, >, or =.

1. 4 _____ 7

2. 12 _____ 8

3. How many teddy bears are left? _____ teddy bears

4. Laurel has 2 dolls. Rosa has 3 dolls. How many dolls do they have in all? _____ dolls

For questions 5–7, circle the digit in the ones place.

5. 19 **6.** 92 **7.** 27

8. Write the missing number. _____

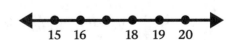

15   16   18   19   20

9. 5 + 4 = _____

10. 9 − 4 = _____

Second-Grade Math Minutes © 2002 Creative Teaching Press

Minute 3

Name _____

1. Write what comes next in the pattern.   2, 4, 6, _____, _____

2. 7 − 5 = _____

3. 2 + 5 = _____

For questions 4 and 5, write the number.

4. nine = _____   **5.** seven = _____

6. 2 + ☐ = 8   **7.** Use <, >, or, =.   12 _____ 9

Use the pictograph to complete questions 8–10.

Ice Cream Children Like Best

Vanilla	🍦 🍦 🍦
Chocolate	🍦 🍦 🍦 🍦 🍦 🍦
Strawberry	🍦 🍦 🍦 🍦

🍦 = 1 child

8. How many children like chocolate ice cream? _____ children

9. Which flavor do children like more—vanilla or strawberry?
_____

10. Circle which flavor children like the most:

strawberry   chocolate   vanilla

Second-Grade Math Minutes © 2002 Creative Teaching Press

Minute 4

Name _____

1. $8 - \boxed{} = 6$

2.   4
       $\underline{+\,3}$

3. Use <, >, or, =.   31 _____ 43

4. Write the missing number.   12, 14, _____, 18, 20

5. 12 children like blue balloons. 8 children like red balloons. Which color balloon do more children like? _____ balloons

For questions 6 and 7, circle the value of the <u>underlined</u> digit.

6. 1<u>5</u>   5   50

7. <u>5</u>2   5   50

8. Write the missing numbers.   _____ and _____

30 31 32 33   35 36 37   39

For questions 9 and 10, circle the name of the shape.

9. ◯   square   circle   triangle

10. ▷   square   circle   triangle

Second-Grade Math Minutes © 2002 Creative Teaching Press

Minute 5

Name _____

1. How many stars in all? ☆ ☆ + ☆ ☆
_____ stars ☆ ☆ ☆ ☆

2. 8 – 3 = _____

For questions 3 and 4, write the number.

3. eleven = _____

4. three = _____

5. 11
    + 13
    _____

6. The clown has 9 balls. He drops 3 balls. How many balls does he have left? _____ balls

7. ☐ + 6 = 9

For questions 8–10, circle the name of the coin.

8.   penny   nickel   dime   quarter

9.   penny   nickel   dime   quarter

10.   penny   nickel   dime   quarter

Second-Grade Math Minutes © 2002 Creative Teaching Press

Minute 6

Name _____

For questions 1–3, write the value of the coin.

1. = _____ ¢

2. = _____ ¢

3. = _____ ¢

4. Write the missing numbers. _____ and _____

50 51 52 53 54   56 57   59 60

5. 22
     + 41

6. 9 + ☐ = 16

7. Find the pattern. Write the missing number.

42, 44, _____, 48, 50

For questions 8–10, count the coins. Write how much money in all.

8. + = _____ ¢

9. + = _____ ¢

10. + = _____ ¢

Second-Grade Math Minutes © 2002 Creative Teaching Press

Minute 7

Name _____

For questions 1–3, use <, >, or, =.

1. 6 _____ 3

2. 12 _____ 18

3. 89 _____ 92

4. This coin is called a <u>nickel</u>.

Circle: True   or   False

For questions 5 and 6, write the number.

5. eight = _____

6. twelve = _____

For questions 7 and 8, find the pattern. Write the missing number.

7. 2, 4, 6, _____, 10, 12

8. 5, 10, _____, 20, 25, 30

9. 9 + 9 = _____

10.   8
    − 5
    ____

Second-Grade Math Minutes © 2002 Creative Teaching Press

Minute 8

Name _____

1. Write the missing numbers. _____ and _____

1 2 3 4   7 8 9 10

2. How many cookies in all?
_____ cookies

3. $6 + \boxed{} = 13$

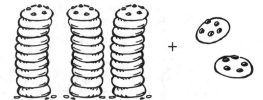

4. Find the pattern.
Write the missing numbers. 5, 10, 15, _____, 25, _____

For questions 5–7, count the coins. Write how much money in all.

5. ⬤ + ⬤ ⬤ ⬤ ⬤ = _____ ¢

6. ⬤ ⬤ + ⬤ = _____ ¢

7. ⬤ ⬤ + ⬤ ⬤ = _____ ¢

8. Clay had 5 toy cars. His dad bought him 8 more. How many toy cars does Clay have in all? _____ cars

9. Use <, >, or, =.   58 _____ 72

10.   9
         -7

Second-Grade Math Minutes © 2002 Creative Teaching Press

Minute 9

Name _____

1. Julia read 4 books. Roger read 5 books. How many books did they read in all? _____ books

2. $3 + \boxed{} = 8$

Use the parade of animals to complete questions 3–5.

3. The lion is <u>first</u> in line.   Circle: True   or   False

4. Which animal is <u>third</u>? _____

5. The parrot is <u>fifth</u> in line.   Circle: True   or   False

6. How many pancakes in all? _____ pancakes

7. $7 + 7 =$ _____

8. $\begin{array}{r} 56 \\ -\ 21 \\ \hline \end{array}$

9. Find the pattern. Write the missing number.   35, 40, 45, _____, 55

10. Draw a circle.

Second-Grade Math Minutes © 2002 Creative Teaching Press

Minute 10

Name _____

1. $4 + 9 = $ _____

2.
$$\begin{array}{r} 25 \\ -\ 11 \\ \hline \end{array}$$

3. Name the shape. _____

4. How much in all?

 $+\ 3¢ = $ _____ ¢

5. ⬜ $-\ 5 = 3$

6. How many blocks in all?
_____ blocks

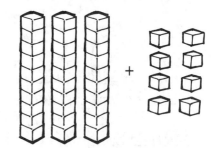

7. Write the number twenty-two. _____

8. Find the pattern. Write the missing number.   _____, 10, 15, 20

9. $11 + 4 = $ _____

10. Draw a square.

Second-Grade Math Minutes © 2002 Creative Teaching Press

Minute 11

Name _____

For questions 1 and 2, write the time.

1. = _____ : _____   **2.** = _____ : _____

3. Find the pattern. Write the missing number.

12, 14, 16, _____, 20

4. Use <, >, or, =.   36 _____ 48

Use the picture to complete questions 5–7.

5. Does the soil cost more or less than the seeds? _____

6. Michele bought soil and seeds. How much did she spend? _____ ¢

7. Aaron has one dime. He wants to buy a watering can. Does he have enough money?

Circle: Yes   or   No

8. Draw a triangle.

For questions 9 and 10, write the number.

9. thirteen = _____   **10.** fifteen = _____

Second-Grade Math Minutes © 2002 Creative Teaching Press

Minute 12

Name _____

1. Find the pattern. Write the missing number.   35, 40, _____, 50, 55

2. 8 − ☐ = 3

For questions 3 and 4, write the time.

3. = _____ : _____

4. = _____ : _____

5. How many blocks in all?
_____ blocks

For questions 6 and 7, write the number.

6. forty-three = _____

7. twenty-nine = _____

8. Use <, >, or, =.   97 _____ 86

9. 12 − 3 = _____

10. 8 gray mice and 10 white mice are playing. How many mice are there in all? _____ mice

Second-Grade Math Minutes © 2002 Creative Teaching Press

Minute 13

Name _____

1. Find the pattern. Write the missing number.
   3, 6, 9, 12, _____, 18

2. Draw the clock hands to show 10:00.

3. 12 + 14 = _____

4. 18 − 8 = _____

For questions 5 and 6, write the number.

5. twenty-two = _____   6. forty-five = _____

Use the picture to complete questions 7–9.

7. What is second in line? _____

8. Is the train fifth or sixth in line? _____

9. What is fourth in line? _____

10. How much money in all?

 + 4¢ = _____ ¢

Second-Grade Math Minutes © 2002 Creative Teaching Press

Minute 14

Name _____

For questions 1 and 2, write how much money in all.

1. ⬤⬤⬤⬤ = _____ ¢

2. ⬤⬤⬤⬤⬤⬤⬤⬤ = _____ ¢

3. Write the number thirty-six. _____

4. Find the pattern. Write the missing number.   3, 6, ____, 12, 15

5. 3 + 2 + 5 = _____

For questions 6 and 7, write the digit in the tens place.

6. 48 _____   **7.** 85 _____

Use the pictograph to complete questions 8–10.

Pond Life

🐢	🐢 🐢
🐟	🐟 🐟 🐟 🐟 🐟
🐸	🐸 🐸 🐸

8. How many fish live in the pond ? _____ fish

9. Do more turtles or frogs live in the pond? _____

10. How many animals in all live in the pond? _____ animals

Second-Grade Math Minutes © 2002 Creative Teaching Press

Minute 15

Name _____

1. Find the pattern. Write the missing number.

15, 18, 21, 24, _____, 30

2.
```
   4
   3
 + 2
```

3.
```
   36
 − 23
```

4. 6 + 11 = _____

5. Write the missing number. 10, 20, 30, _____, 50, 60.

For questions 6 and 7, write the time.

6.  = _____

7. = _____

For questions 8–10, write the number of tens and ones.

8. 36 = _____ tens _____ ones

9. 52 = _____ tens _____ ones

10. 49 = _____ tens _____ ones

Second-Grade Math Minutes © 2002 Creative Teaching Press

Minute 16

Name _____

For questions 1–3, circle the name of the shape.

1. ⬭ circle   triangle   rectangle   oval

2. ▭ circle   triangle   rectangle   oval

3. △ circle   triangle   rectangle   oval

4. Find the pattern. Write the missing number.

68, 70, 72, _____, 76, 78

Use the pictograph to complete questions 5–7.

 = **one child**

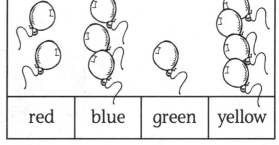

Balloons Sold

| red | blue | green | yellow |

5. How many children bought yellow balloons? _____ children

6. Did children buy more red balloons or blue balloons? _____ balloons

7. How many balloons were sold in all? _____ balloons

8. Carlos has 6 marbles. William has 3 marbles. Pat has 2 marbles. How many marbles do they have altogether? _____ marbles

9. Write the number sixty-eight. _____

10. Draw a rectangle.

Second-Grade Math Minutes © 2002 Creative Teaching Press

Minute 17

Name _____

1. Tyler has 5 pencils. Ben gives him 8 more pencils. How many pencils does Tyler have in all? _____ pencils

For questions 2 and 3, write how much money in all.

2. = _____ ¢

3. = _____ ¢

4.
$$\begin{array}{r} 4 \\ 3 \\ + 5 \\ \hline \end{array}$$

5. How many pennies are there? _____ pennies

For questions 6 and 7, write the number of tens and ones.

6. 49 = _____ tens _____ ones

7. 94 = _____ tens _____ ones

8. 9 + 8 = _____

9. Write the missing number.   42, 45, 48, _____, 54, 57

10. 46 > 39   Circle: True   or   False

Second-Grade Math Minutes © 2002 Creative Teaching Press

Minute 18

Name _____

1. 56
   + 23
   —————

2. Write the missing number.   35, 40, _____, 50, 55

3. 9 + 9 = _____

For questions 4 and 5, write the time.

4.  = _____

5. = _____

6. Write the number fifty-six. _____

7. 5 + ☐ + 2 = 9

For questions 8 and 9, circle the greater number.

8. 76   67

9. 50   53

10. Name the shape. _____ ☐

Second-Grade Math Minutes © 2002 Creative Teaching Press

Minute 19

Name _____

Use the pictograph to complete questions 1–3.

Wear Glasses	Don't Wear Glasses

1. How many children wear glasses?
_____ children

2. Most children wear glasses.

Circle: True   or   False

3. How many children don't
wear glasses? _____ children

4.   32
       +13
       ‾‾‾‾

5.   47
       − 35
       ‾‾‾‾

For questions 6 and 7, circle the greater number.

6.   53   45

7.   47   74

For questions 8 and 9, write the missing number.

8.   40, 50, 60, _____, 80, 90

9.   36, 39, _____, 45, 48

10. Name the shape. _____

Second-Grade Math Minutes © 2002 Creative Teaching Press

Minute 20

Name _____

1. $5 + 12 =$ _____

2. Mason has 4 cars. Rhonda has 5 cars. How many cars do they have altogether? _____ cars

3.
$$\begin{array}{r} 3 \\ 3 \\ +\ 4 \\ \hline \end{array}$$

For questions 4 and 5, write the value of the underlined digit.

4. 8<u>9</u>   _____

5. <u>2</u>3   _____

6. Write the missing number.   86, 87, 88, _____, 90, 91

7. Write how much money in all.

 = _____ ¢

8. Write the number seventy-three. _____

For questions 9 and 10, use <, >, or, =.

9. 87 _____ 78

10. 54 _____ 60

Second-Grade Math Minutes © 2002 Creative Teaching Press

Minute 21

Name _____

For questions 1 and 2, write the doubles. Add.

1.  _____ + _____ = _____

2. _____ + _____ = _____

3. Skip count by 2. Write the missing odd number.   1, 3, 5, _____, 9, 11

Use the picture to complete questions 4–6.

A   B   C   D   E   F

4. Draw a circle around the bird that is fourth.

5. Draw an X over the bird that is second.

6. Draw a box around the bird that is sixth.

For questions 7 and 8, circle the coins you need to buy the food.

7. 18¢

8. 20¢

9. Write the number twenty-eight. _____

10. Draw the clock hands to show 2:00.

Second-Grade Math Minutes © 2002 Creative Teaching Press

Minute 22

Name _____

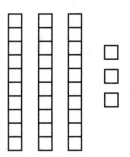

1. Draw an oval.

2. How many squares in all? _____ squares

For questions 3 and 4, circle the coin of greater value.

3.   **4.**

5.   16
       + 3
       ‾‾‾

6. $19 - \boxed{} = 10$

7. Write the missing number. 21, 24, _____, 30, 33

For questions 8 and 9, write the doubles. Add.

8. _____ + _____ = _____

9. _____ + _____ = _____

10. Draw a triangle.

Second-Grade Math Minutes © 2002 Creative Teaching Press

Minute 23

Name _____

1. 55
   + 24

2. ☐ + 14 = 18

3. Complete the fact family.   8 + 7 = 15   15 – _____ = 7

         7 + 8 = 15   15 – 7 = 8

4. Skip count by 2. Write the missing even number.
        42, 44, _____, 48, 50

5. Write the time. _____

6. 24
        – 13

7. Adam has 8 stamps. Hayley has 6 stamps. How many more
        stamps does Adam have than Hayley? _____ stamps

8. Circle the number that is less: 8   18

9. Write the missing number.
        63, 66, 69, _____, 75

10. Write the number ninety-nine. _____

Second-Grade Math Minutes © 2002 Creative Teaching Press

Minute 24

Name _____

1. 3 + 7 + 8 = _____

2. Add the double numbers.   8 + 8 = _____

3.   17
      + 18

4. Draw the clock hands to show 12:30.

For questions 5–7, write the number that comes after.

5. 67 _____

6. 19 _____

7. 74 _____

8. Circle the even number: 11   14   19

9. Write the number of tens and ones.

79 = _____ tens   _____ ones

10. How much money in all? _____ ¢

Second-Grade Math Minutes © 2002 Creative Teaching Press

Minute 25

Name _____

1. 2, 4, 6, and 8 are odd numbers.   Circle: True   or   False

2. Complete the fact family. $9 + 4 = 13$ _____ $- 9 = 4$

   $4 + 9 = 13$ $13 - 4 = 9$

3.   34
     + 47
     ‾‾‾‾

4. Kyra found 4 insects. Jamie found 6 insects. Ruth found 2 insects. How many insects did they find in all? _____ insects

5. Circle the name of the shape:

   square   rectangle   diamond

6. $17 -$ ⬜ $= 9$

7. Write the time. _____

8. Write the number seventeen. _____

9. Circle the number that is less: 94   49

10. Write the missing number.

   _____, 30, 40, 50, 60

Second-Grade Math Minutes © 2002 Creative Teaching Press

Minute 26

Name _____

1. Complete the fact family.

2. $4 + \boxed{} = 7$

$9 + 5 = 14$ $14 - 5 = 9$

$5 + \underline{\hspace{1cm}} = 14$ $14 - 9 = 5$

For questions 3 and 4, write the missing number.

3. 30, _____, 36, 39, 42   **4.** 40, _____, 60, 70, 80

Use the bar graph to complete questions 5–7.

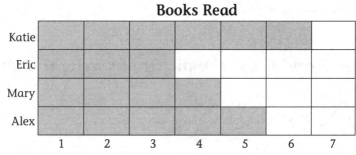

5. Who read four books? _____

6. Who read the most books? _____

7. How many more books did Alex read than Eric? _____ more books

8. Write the number thirty-five. _____

9. 17
     − 9

10. 12
      + 9

Second-Grade Math Minutes © 2002 Creative Teaching Press

Minute 27

Name _____

1. Write the time. _____

2. Write the number sixty-eight. _____

3. Draw the clock hands to show 9:00.

4. 17
   + 8
   ____

5. Skip count. Write the missing odd number.
   53, 55, _____, 59, 61

6. 10
   − 7
   ____

For questions 7 and 8, use the picture to write the number sentence.

7.   _____ + _____ = _____

8.    _____ + _____ = _____

9. Write the name of the coin. _____

10. Sam has 9 games. Alina has 3 games less than Sam. How many games does Alina have? _____ games

Second-Grade Math Minutes © 2002 Creative Teaching Press

Minute 28

Name _____

1. Skip count. Write the missing even number.   64, _____ , 68, 70, 72

2. How many pennies in all?
_____ pennies

3.   83
      + 13

4.   17
      − 8

5. Write the time. _____

6. Tyler has 5 robots. He gets 4 more robots for his birthday. How many robots does Tyler have in all? _____ robots

7. 6 + 4 > 4 + 4   Circle: True   or   False

For questions 8 and 9, draw the minute and hour hands.
Write the time.

8. _____

9. _____

10. Complete the fact family.   7 + 5 =12   12 − _____ = 7

5 + 7 = 12   12 − 7 = 5

Second-Grade Math Minutes © 2002 Creative Teaching Press

Minute 29

Name _____

1. Write the time. _____

2. Write the number thirty-three. _____

For questions 3 and 4, circle the digit in the tens place.

3. 68   **4.**   86

5. How many months are in 1 year? _____ months

6. 16 + 2 = _____

For questions 7 and 8, use < or >.

7.

8.

9. 14 − 6 = _____

10. Write the missing number.

_____, 60, 70, 80, 90

Second-Grade Math Minutes © 2002 Creative Teaching Press

Minute 30

Name _____

1. Circle the name of the first month of the year:

      May   December   February   January

2.
$$\begin{array}{r} 24 \\ -\ 8 \\ \hline \end{array}$$

3. Tabby has 8 kittens. Bootsie has 5 kittens. How many more kittens does Tabby have than Bootsie? _____ kittens

4. Write the time. _____

For questions 5 and 6, write the words in order.

5. second first third _____

6. fifth sixth fourth _____

For questions 7 and 8, circle the greater number.

7. 89   98   **8.** 33   13

9. Write the number eighty-five. _____

10. Circle the rectangle: □   △   ▭

Second-Grade Math Minutes © 2002 Creative Teaching Press

Minute 31

Name _____

1. Draw the hour and minute hands to show 3:15.

Use the bar graph to complete questions 2 and 3.

Children's Eye Color

	1	2	3	4	5	6	7	8	9	10	11
blue											
brown											

2. How many children have brown eyes? _____ children

3. Do more children have blue eyes or brown eyes? _____ eyes

4. 16
      + 8
      —————

5. Keesha has 15 books. She has read 11 of the books. How many books didn't she read? _____ books

6. How much money in all? _____ ¢

7. 6 + 6 + 6 = _____

8. Circle the number that is less: 45   52

9. Write the next odd number.   3, 5, 7, 9, _____

10. Circle the correct order of months:

April June July   October November December

Second-Grade Math Minutes © 2002 Creative Teaching Press

38

Minute 32

Name _____

1.   24
      + 6
      ——

2.   Circle the number that is less: 78   88

For questions 3 and 4, circle the digit in the ones place.

3. 68   **4.**   23

5. <u>Underline</u> the correct time.

    3:15   3:25   3:30

6. A rectangle has 4 sides.   Circle :   True   or   False

7.   12
      + 22
      ——

8. Alfredo has 15 computer games. He bought 5 more games.
    How many games does he have in all? _____ games

9.   54
      − 15
      ——

10. What is the last month of the year? _____

Second-Grade Math Minutes © 2002 Creative Teaching Press

Minute 33

Name _____

1. Circle the month that comes next after March:

February   April   May

2. Tim has 10 boats. Adam has 12 boats. How many boats do they have altogether? _____ boats

For questions 3 and 4, circle the correct time.

3.  4:15   4:30   4:45

4.   5:30   6:25   6:30

5. Use + or − to make the sentence true.   8 _____ 6 = 2

6.   52
       + 42
       _____

7.   37
       − 12
       _____

8. Write the number of tens and ones.   89 = _____ tens _____ ones

9. Write how much money in all. _____ ¢

10. Write the number twelve. _____

Second-Grade Math Minutes © 2002 Creative Teaching Press

Minute 34

Name _____

1. 6 + 3 + 5 = _____

2. Write the number fifteen. _____

3. A square has 3 sides.   Circle: True   or   False

Use the pictograph to complete questions 4 and 5.

Children with or without Brothers and Sisters

brothers	☺ ☺ ☺ ☺ ☺
sisters	☺ ☺ ☺ ☺ ☺ ☺
no brothers/sisters	☺ ☺ ☺

4. Do more children have brothers or sisters? _____

5. How many children have no brothers or sisters? _____ children

6. 18 + 2 = _____

7. Circle the correct time:

   9:45   9:50   9:55

8. In the number 56, which digit is in the ones place? _____

9.   15
    − 7

10.   74
     + 14

Second-Grade Math Minutes © 2002 Creative Teaching Press

Minute 35

Name _____

1. Write the time. _____

2.   23
    + 25

3. Write the missing number.   35, 40, _____, 50, 55

4. Use + or – to make the sentence true.   3 _____ 8 = 11

5.   3
    4
   + 6

6. In the number 34, which digit is in the tens place? _____

7. Write the number of tens and ones.   78 = _____ tens _____ ones

8. Frank has 8 pennies. Shasta has 9 pennies. How many pennies do they have altogether? _____ pennies

9.   89
   – 41

10. Write the number seventy-eight. _____

Second-Grade Math Minutes © 2002 Creative Teaching Press

Minute 36

Name _____

1.   46
         + 28
         ——

2.   Write the missing even number.   _____, 4, 6, 8, 10

3.   Write how much money in all. _____ ¢

For questions 4 and 5, circle the name of the shape.

4.   triangle   square   circle

5.   circle   rectangle   square

6.   Write the time. _____

7.   58
         – 12
         ——

8.   Use + or – to make the sentence true.   18 _____ 4 = 14

9.   Draw a circle around 10 more than 39.   29   49   59

10.   Draw a box around the digit in the tens place.   98

Second-Grade Math Minutes © 2002 Creative Teaching Press

Minute 37

Name _____

Use the days of the week to complete questions 1–3.

Sunday   Monday   Tuesday   Wednesday   Thursday   Friday   Saturday

1. What day comes next after Wednesday?_____

2. What is the seventh day of the week? _____

3. What is the third day of the week? _____

4. $85 + 10 =$ _____

5. $34 - 10 =$ _____

6. Circle the digit in the ones place: 35

7. Write the missing odd number.   51, _____, 55, 57, 59

Use the pictograph to complete questions 8–10.

Popcorn Sales

1st Grade	🍿🍿🍿🍿
= 5 boxes 2nd Grade	🍿🍿🍿🍿🍿🍿
3rd Grade	🍿🍿🍿🍿🍿

8. One picture equals how many real boxes of popcorn?
_____ boxes

9. How many boxes did Grade 2 sell? _____ boxes

10. Which grade sold 20 boxes of popcorn?   Circle: 1st   2nd   3rd

Second-Grade Math Minutes © 2002 Creative Teaching Press

Minute 38

Name _____

1. A triangle has 3 sides and 3 corners.   Circle: True   or   False

2. Circle the figure that is the same size and shape as the shaded figure:

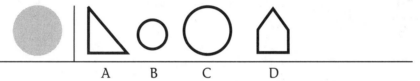

3. Use + or − to make the sentence true.   5 _____ 4 = 9

Use the pictures to complete questions 4 and 5.

4. 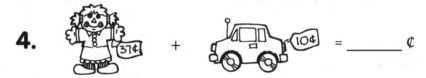 = _____ ¢

5. = _____ ¢

6. Circle the digit in the tens place: 67

7.   12   **8.**   36
        − 11   + 16

9. Write the number of tens and ones.   48 = _____ tens _____ ones

10. Write the number ninety-nine. _____

Second-Grade Math Minutes © 2002 Creative Teaching Press

Minute 39

Name _____

1. Write the missing number.   101, 102, 103, _____, 105

2.   64
       +27

3. Use <, >, or =.   56 _____ 56

4. Circle the digit in the ones place: 49

5. A square has 4 sides and 2 corners.   Circle: True   or   False

6. Write the time. _____

7.   49   **8.**   68 – 31 = _____
        20
       + 27

Use the pictograph to complete questions 9–10.

Vacation Activities

Camping	☺	☺	☺	☺	☺	☺	☺
Fishing	☺	☺	☺	☺			
Biking	☺	☺	☺	☺			

☺ = 1 child

9. How many children went camping? _____ children

10. Which two activities did an equal number of children do?
_____ and _____

Second-Grade Math Minutes © 2002 Creative Teaching Press

Minute 40

Name _____

1. How many corners does a triangle have? _____ corners

2. Circle the name of the shape:

      rectangle   pentagon   hexagon

3. Circle the digit in the ones place: 564

4. John has one quarter and one dime. How much money does he have in all? _____ ¢

5. 65 + 10 = _____

6. Write the missing number.   164, 165, 166, 167, _____

7. Do 12 inches equal 1 foot?   Circle: Yes   or   No

For questions 8 and 9, write the number that comes before.

8. _____   40

9. _____   89

10.   92
       + 57
       ———

Second-Grade Math Minutes © 2002 Creative Teaching Press

Minute 41

Name _____

1. 63 + 20 = _____

2. The tank has 8 fish. 4 of the fish are yellow. How many fish are not yellow? _____ fish

For questions 3 and 4, write the length of each object.

3. _____ inches

4. _____ inches

5. 2 + 6 + 7 = _____

6. Draw the clock hands to show 3:00.

7. Cameron has 18 blue straws and 32 red straws. How many straws does he have in all? _____ straws

8. Write the missing number. 129, _____, 131, 132, 133

9. Write how many groups of 100 there are. _____ groups

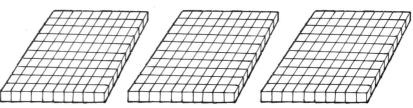

10. 68
    − 10

Second-Grade Math Minutes © 2002 Creative Teaching Press

Minute 42

Name _____

1. Circle the name of the shape:

   pentagon   hexagon   octagon

2. Write the missing number.   149, 150, _____, 152, 153

3.   61
      − 46

4. Sharon saw 12 birds. Kari saw 17 birds. How many birds did they see altogether? _____ birds

5. Write the time. _____

6.   22
      + 66

7. Circle the digit in the tens place: 28

8. Circle the digit in the hundreds place: 873

9. Write how many hundreds there are. _____ hundreds

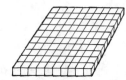 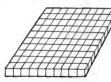 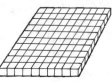 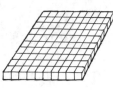 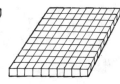

10. How many days are in 1 week? _____ days

Second-Grade Math Minutes © 2002 Creative Teaching Press

Minute 43

Name _____

1. Circle the name of the shape:

[rectangle]   circle   rectangle   square

2. Write 10 less than 89. _____

3. Circle the digit in the hundreds place: 375

4. 93 – 40 = _____

5. Use <, >, or, =.   67 _____ 87

6.   621
     + 230

7.   71
      – 35

In questions 8 and 9, which shapes have matching parts when they are folded on the line? Circle the answer.

8.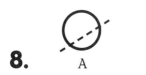
   A   B   C

9.
   A   B   C

10. Write how much money in all. _____ ¢

Second-Grade Math Minutes © 2002 Creative Teaching Press

Minute 44

Name _____

1. Write the number one hundred seventy-four. _____

2.
$$\begin{array}{r} 200 \\ -\ 100 \\ \hline \end{array}$$

3. $75 - \boxed{} = 34$

4. Circle the digit in the ones place: 61

5.
$$\begin{array}{r} 96 \\ +\ 55 \\ \hline \end{array}$$

6. Draw the clock hands to show 5:55.

For questions 7 and 8, circle what you would use to measure each.

7. length of your classroom   inches   feet

8. width of this sheet of paper   inches   feet

Use the pictograph to complete questions 9 and 10.

Children's Hair Color

blond	☺ ☺ ☺ ☺ ☺
brown	☺ ☺ ☺ ☺ ☺ ☺
red	☺ ☺ ☺

☺ = 2 children

9. How many children have blond hair? _____ children

10. How many children have red hair? _____ children

Second-Grade Math Minutes © 2002 Creative Teaching Press

Minute 45

Name _____

1. 84 − 30 = _____

2.
$$\begin{array}{r} 300 \\ -\ 100 \\ \hline \end{array}$$

3. Write the number six hundred thirty. _____

4. Circle the digit in the hundreds place: 921

For questions 5 and 6, write how many inches long each object is.

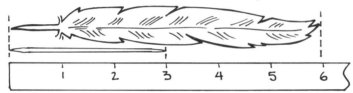

5. The feather is _____ inches long.

6. The toothpick is _____ inches long.

7. 4 + 6 + 8 = _____

8. Write what the time will be 1 hour after. _____

Use the picture to complete questions 9 and 10.

9. How much money does Amy have? _____ ¢

10. Who has more money? _____

Amy

Evan

Second-Grade Math Minutes © 2002 Creative Teaching Press

Minute 46

Name _____

1.   404
    +114
    ———

2.   Use + or − to make the sentence true.   45 _____ 21 = 24

3.   A bathtub is shorter than 1 foot.   Circle: True   or   False

4.   How many sides does a triangle have? _____ sides

5.   558
    − 200
    ———

6.   Write what the time was 1 hour <u>before</u>. _____

7.   4 + 7 + 9 = _____

For questions 8 and 9, circle the coins you need to buy each.

8. 

9.

10.   Write the missing numbers.

   136, _____, 138, 139, 140, _____, _____

Second-Grade Math Minutes © 2002 Creative Teaching Press

Minute 47

Name _____

1. James lost 2 dimes and 5 pennies. How much money did he lose?
_____ ¢

2. ☐ − 14 = 8

3. Write what the time will be 2 hours <u>after</u>. _____

4. 458 = _____ hundreds _____ tens _____ ones

5.
$$\begin{array}{r} 85 \\ -\ 29 \\ \hline \end{array}$$

6. Write the missing odd numbers.
65, _____, 69, 71, 73, _____

7.
$$\begin{array}{r} 82 \\ +\ 14 \\ \hline \end{array}$$

8. Milo has 15 keys. Sarah has 8 keys. How many more keys does Milo have than Sarah? _____ keys

9. Circle the digit in the tens place: 193

10.
$$\begin{array}{r} 4 \\ 5 \\ +\ 3 \\ \hline \end{array}$$

Second-Grade Math Minutes © 2002 Creative Teaching Press

Minute 48

Name _____

1. Circle the number with a 3 in the tens place: 132   321   23

2. Draw a box around the month that comes right before June.

April   July   May

For questions 3 and 4, circle *Yes* or *No*.

3. Is a bar of soap shorter than 1 foot?   Yes   No

4. Is a flagpole taller than 1 foot?   Yes   No

5. Write what the time was 2 hours <u>before</u>. _____

6. 22 + ☐ = 32

Use the picture to complete questions 7 and 8.

Tom   Sharon

7. How much money does Sharon have? _____ ¢

8. Who has <u>less</u> money? _____

9. 8 + 9 + 5 = _____

10. Write the name of the shape. _____

Second-Grade Math Minutes © 2002 Creative Teaching Press

Minute 49

Name _____

1. Circle the number that has an 8 in the ones place:

879   978   897

2. Write the missing numbers.

149, 150, _____, 152, _____, _____

3.
$$92$$
$$-\ 79$$

4. 6 + 3 + 8 = _____

Use the menu to complete questions 5 and 6.

Lunch Menu	
juice 15¢	sandwich 35¢
milk 12¢	pizza 42¢

5. Which costs more—pizza or a sandwich? _____

6. Mike bought juice and pizza. How much did he spend? _____ ¢

7. 44 + 30 = _____

Use the letters to complete questions 8–10.

A   B   C   D   E   F   G   H   I   J

8. The fourth letter is _____.   **9.** The ninth letter is _____.

10. The seventh letter is _____.

Second-Grade Math Minutes © 2002 Creative Teaching Press

Minute 50

Name _____

1.   15
        + 30

2. Circle the number that has six ones:

   165   56   68

3.   6
         2
       + 2

4.   849
        − 130

In questions 5 and 6, circle the time each clock shows.

5.    4:45   4:50   4:55

6.    7:30   7:35   7:40

7. Write the missing numbers.   _____, 187, 188, _____, 190

8.   946
        − 317

9. A square has 4 sides and 8 corners.   Circle: True   or   False

10. What would you use to measure a tree?   Circle: inches   or   feet

Second-Grade Math Minutes © 2002 Creative Teaching Press

Minute 51

Name _____

1. Write how many hours have passed.
   _____ hours

2. 3
    7
  + 5

3. 74 − ☐ = 22

For questions 4 and 5, write how many centimeters long each object is.

4. 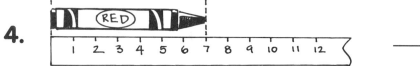 _____cm

5. 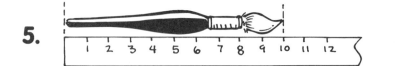 _____cm

6. Write the missing even numbers.

   88, 90, _____, 94, 96, _____, 100

7. 41
  − 38

Use the pictograph to complete questions 8–10.

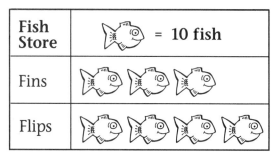

8. How many fish does equal? _____ fish

9. Skip count. How many fish are in Fins? _____ fish

10. How many more fish are in Flips than are in Fins? _____ fish

Second-Grade Math Minutes © 2002 Creative Teaching Press

Minute 52

Name _____

1.   56
        − 34

2.   8 + 4 + 8 = _____

3.   How many blocks are there?

Circle: 131   or   113

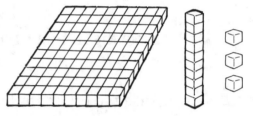

4.   Write the next number.   398, 399, _____

5.   Circle the digit in the ones place: 342

6.   Write the number seven hundred thirty-five. _____

7.   Write how many hours have passed.

      _____ hours

8.   100 centimeters equals 1 meter.   Circle: True   or   False

9.   How many hours do most children sleep each night?
        Circle the answer.   10 hours   30 hours

10.   A square has 4 sides all the same length.   Circle: True   or   False

Second-Grade Math Minutes © 2002 Creative Teaching Press

Minute 53

Name _____

1.   772
       − 555

2.   85
        + 14

3.   Circle the number that is 10 greater than 451:   551   461

4.   Circle the figure that is the same size and shape as the shaded figure:

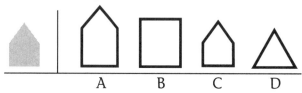

5.   Write the missing number.   100, 200, 300, 400, _____

6.   Add to find the distance around the shape.

       _____

For questions 7 and 8, circle the name of the shape.

7.   sphere   cube   cone

8.   sphere   cube   cylinder

9.   Underline the digit in the hundreds place.   487

10.   Are all of these even numbers?   Circle: Yes or No
        102, 103, 104, 106, 108

Second-Grade Math Minutes © 2002 Creative Teaching Press

Minute 54

Name _____

1. Circle the name of the solid:

   cone   cube   rectangular prism

2. Underline the digit in the hundreds place.   352

3. 70 – 16 = _____

4. Write the missing numbers. 400, 500, _____, 700, 800, _____

In questions 5 and 6, which shapes have matching parts when they are folded on the line? Circle the answer.

5.

6.

7. 7 + 5 + 8 = _____

8. Circle the greater amount:

9. Write the missing odd number.
   121, 123, 125, 127, _____

10. 41
     28
    +31

Second-Grade Math Minutes © 2002 Creative Teaching Press

Minute 55

Name _____

1. Are these all odd numbers?   Circle: Yes   or   No
121, 123, 125, 127, 129

2. Add to find the distance around the shape.

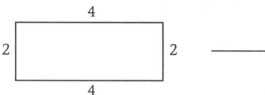

3.   56
        + 98

4. Stacy walked for 30 minutes. Write what time she stopped.

Starting Time   Stopping Time _____

5. Write the missing numbers.   _____, 500, 600, _____, 800

6. How much money in all? _____ ¢

7.   707
        + 167

8. Circle the shape that shows a line of symmetry:

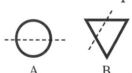

A   B   C

9. November comes next after December.   Circle: True   or   False

10.   640
         − 131

Second-Grade Math Minutes © 2002 Creative Teaching Press

Minute 56

Name _____

1. 165
   + 494

2. Is this a line of symmetry?   Circle: Yes or No

3. Write the number nine hundred sixty-six. _____

4. The month that comes right before October is November.
   Circle: True or False

5. Write the missing even numbers. 124, 126, 128, _____, 132, _____

6. Circle the number that has 8 in the tens place:

   893   938   983

7. The distance around a shape is called the perimeter.
   Circle: True or False

8. 58
   + 27

For questions 9 and 10, circle the name of the solid.

9.   cylinder   cone   rectangular prism

10.   cube   cone   rectangular prism

Second-Grade Math Minutes © 2002 Creative Teaching Press

Minute 57

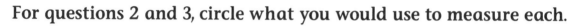

Name _____

1. Is this a line of symmetry?   Circle: Yes   or   No

For questions 2 and 3, circle what you would use to measure each.

2. length of a car   inches   feet

3. height of a tree   inches   feet

4. Juni cleaned for 30 minutes. Write what time he stopped.

Starting Time   Stopping Time _____

5.   464
      – 127

6.   143
      + 372

7. Write the missing numbers.
100, _____, 300, _____, 500, 600, 700

8.   33
      + 82

9.   22
        19
      + 50

10. Circle the number with 2 in the tens place:

525   255   552

Second-Grade Math Minutes © 2002 Creative Teaching Press

Minute 58

Name _____

1. A rectangle has 4 sides and 4 corners.   Circle: True   or   False

2. Draw a line of symmetry through the shape.

3. 473
   −136

4. 56
   + 27

For questions 5 and 6, write the length of each.

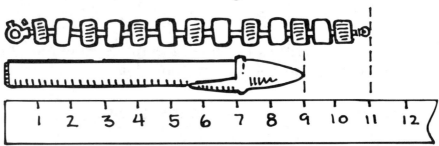

5. The bracelet is _____ centimeters long.

6. The pen is _____ centimeters long.

7. Write the number five hundred fifteen. _____

8. John is 46 inches tall. How tall will he be if he grows 5 inches?
   _____ inches

9. Circle the greater number: 259   356

10. Circle the value of the coins:

       60¢   70¢   80¢

Second-Grade Math Minutes © 2002 Creative Teaching Press

Minute 59

Name _____

1.
619
− 401

2.
16
+ 10

3. Write the number of hundreds, tens, and ones.

248 = _____ hundreds _____ tens _____ ones

4. Write the number that comes between.   780 _____ 782

5. Use < or >.   675 _____ 657

6. Kayla has 8 pennies. Ian has 24 pennies. How many pennies do they have altogether? _____ pennies

7. Write the number seven hundred twelve. _____

For questions 8 and 9, circle what you would use to measure each.

8. length of a paper clip   centimeters   meters

9. height of a ladder   centimeters   meters

10. Write what the time will be 3 hours later.

 _____

Second-Grade Math Minutes © 2002 Creative Teaching Press

Minute 60

Name _____

1. Circle the shape that does not show a line of symmetry:

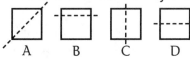

A   B   C   D

2.
$$\begin{array}{r} 468 \\ -\ 139 \\ \hline \end{array}$$

3. Write the number four hundred thirty-one. _____

4.
$$\begin{array}{r} 35 \\ +\ 10 \\ \hline \end{array}$$

5. Write the name of the shape. _____

6. Circle the value of the coins:

    36¢   41¢   43¢

7. Write the number that comes between.   789 _____ 791

8. Write the missing numbers.

500, _____, 700, 800, _____, 1000

9. Write the time. _____

10. Write the missing odd number.

977, 979, _____, 983, 985

Second-Grade Math Minutes © 2002 Creative Teaching Press

Minute 61

Name _____

1. 354
       − 251

2. Write the name of the shape. _____

For questions 3 and 4, circle what you would use to measure each.

3. length of a swimming pool   centimeters   meters

4. height of a box of cereal   centimeters   meters

5. 563 = _____ hundreds _____ tens _____ ones

6.   43   **7.**   74
        + 10   15
                           + 12

8. 3 + 3 + 3 = ☐   ⊡ + ⊡ + ⊡

9. Write the number that comes between.   198 _____ 200

10. Circle the value of the money:

$1.00 $10.00 $100.00

Second-Grade Math Minutes © 2002 Creative Teaching Press

Minute 62

Name _____

1. Gina went to her dance class at 4:00. The class was 1 hour long. What time did the class stop? _____

2. 164
   + 249

3. What would you use to measure a soccer field?

   Circle: centimeters   or   meters

4. Draw an X over the circle.

   ◯   ⊕

5. 64
   − 59

6. Use + or − to make the sentence true.   34 ____ 21 = 13

7. Ben started his project on Tuesday. He finished three days later. What day did he finish? _____

8. Circle the value of the coins:

   77¢   87¢   97¢

9. 4 + 4 + 4 = ☐   ☆☆ ☆☆ + ☆☆ ☆☆ + ☆☆ ☆☆

10. 697 = _____ hundreds _____ tens _____ ones

Second-Grade Math Minutes © 2002 Creative Teaching Press

Minute 63

Name _____

1. Write the numbers that come before and after.
   _____ 789 _____

2.   45
     + 10
     ——

3. Write how many eggs are in one dozen. _____ eggs

Use the pictograph to complete questions 4–6.

Flower Sales	
Monday	🌸🌸🌸
Tuesday	🌸🌸🌸🌸
Wednesday	🌸
Thursday	🌸🌸🌸🌸🌸
Friday	🌸🌸🌸

🌸 = 10 flowers

4. How many flowers were sold on Tuesday? _____ flowers

5. Which two days sold the same number of flowers? _____ and _____

6. Which day sold the least flowers? _____

7. 632 = _____ hundreds _____ tens _____ ones

8. 2 + 2 + 2 + 2 = ☐   ○○ + ○○ + ○○ + ○○

9. Circle the cylinder: ▭ ⬚
   A   B

10. Write the day that comes next after Saturday. _____

Second-Grade Math Minutes © 2002 Creative Teaching Press

Minute 64

Name _____

1. 420 = _____ hundreds _____ tens _____ ones

2. Circle the number with the fewest hundreds:

   415   307   612

For questions 3 and 4, circle what you need to equal 25¢.

3.   4.

5. Find the pattern. Write the missing number.
   770, 775, 780, 785, _____

6.   38
   + 53

7.   46
   + 10

8.   284
   − 149

9. Write the perimeter of the shape. _____

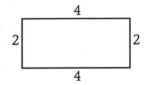

10. Write the time. _____

Second-Grade Math Minutes © 2002 Creative Teaching Press

Minute 65

Name _____

1. Circle the greater number:
359   395

2. 80 + 10 = _____

3. Nancy has 16¢. Randy has 7¢ less than Nancy. How much money does Randy have? _____ ¢

4. Write how much money in all. _____ ¢

5. Megan has one dozen cars. How many cars is that? _____ cars

6. Use < or >.   851 _____ 815

7. 3 + 3 + 3 + 3 = ⬜   ☆☆ + ☆☆ + ☆☆ + ☆☆
                         ☆   ☆   ☆   ☆

8. Jana needs 10 centimeters of ribbon. Circle the ribbon she needs.

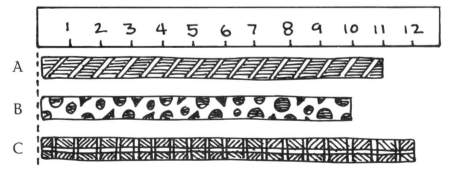

9. Write the number four hundred thirty-eight. _____

10. Write how many hours have passed. _____ hours

Second-Grade Math Minutes © 2002 Creative Teaching Press

Minute 66

Name _____

1. In the number 298, which digit is in the ones place? _____

2.
$$
\begin{array}{r}
688 \\
+\ 427 \\
\hline
\end{array}
$$

3. Write the perimeter. _____

4.
$$
\begin{array}{r}
74 \\
-\ 16 \\
\hline
\end{array}
$$

5. Is this a line of symmetry?   Circle: Yes   or   No

6. Is this a cube or a cylinder? _____

7. $83 + 10 =$ _____

8. Evan has 37¢. Candice has 8¢ less than Evan. How much money does Candice have? _____ ¢

For questions 9 and 10, write the correct letter to spell the money words.

a   e   i   o   u

9. nick ___ l

10. doll ___ r

Second-Grade Math Minutes © 2002 Creative Teaching Press

Minute 67

Name _____

1. Dad has one dozen eggs. He uses 6 eggs for breakfast. How many eggs are left?

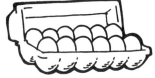

_____ eggs

2.
```
  761
- 652
```

3.
```
  577
+ 482
```

4. Is this a rectangle or a rectangular prism?

_____

5. Use < or >.   265 _____ 256

6. $5 + 5 + 5 =$ ☐   𝗜𝗜𝗜𝗜 + 𝗜𝗜𝗜𝗜 + 𝗜𝗜𝗜𝗜

7. Circle how much money in all: $1.21 $1.16

8. Write the number that comes between.   454 _____ 456

For questions 9 and 10, circle what might happen on a hot summer day.

9. Children build snowmen.   not happen / will happen

10. Ice cream melts outside.   not happen / will happen

Second-Grade Math Minutes © 2002 Creative Teaching Press

Minute 68

Name _____

1. Circle how much money in all:
   $2.23 $2.33 $2.43

2. 89 + 10 = _____

3. Write how many hours have passed.
   _____ hours

4. 56 + 40 = _____

5. Use < or >. $2.35 _____ $2.53

6. Is this shape a square or a cube? _____

Use the table of tallies to
complete questions 7 and 8.

Children's Favorite Books

Tall Tales	IIII IIII III
Fantasy	IIII IIII

7. How many children like fantasy books? _____ children

8. What is the most favorite kind of books? _____

9. Is this a line of symmetry?   Circle: Yes   or   No

10. In the number 563, which digit is in the tens place? _____

Second-Grade Math Minutes © 2002 Creative Teaching Press

Minute 69

Name _____

1. Find the pattern. Write the missing number.
102, _____, 108, 111, 114

2. Circle the greater number: 753   573

3. 36 + 50 = _____

4. Is the circle divided into 4 equal parts?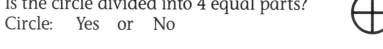
Circle: Yes   or   No

5.   632
   − 315

6. A triangle has 3 sides and 4 corners.   Circle: Yes   or   No

For questions 7 and 8, circle what might happen on a cold winter day.

7. Children will wear swimming suits outside.

   not happen / will happen

8. Children will wear warm clothes outside.

   not happen / will happen

9. A school bus is longer than 1 meter.   Circle: True   or   False

10. 2 + 2 + 2 = ☐

Second-Grade Math Minutes © 2002 Creative Teaching Press

Minute 70

Name _____

1. How long is the paintbrush? _____ cm

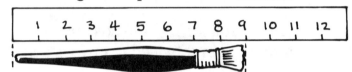

2. Circle the number that is less: 298   689

3. Draw a line of symmetry on the shape.

4. 4 + 4 + 4 + 4 = _____   ⬭⬭ + ⬭⬭ + ⬭⬭ + ⬭⬭

5. Circle the time:
   1:25   7:25

6. Is the circle divided into 4 equal parts?
   Circle: Yes   or   No

7. In the number 328, which digit is in the hundreds place? _____

8. Claude picks a half-dozen apples. How many apples did he pick?
   _____ apples

9.   58
        − 29

10.   Use < or >.   789 _____ 798

Second-Grade Math Minutes © 2002 Creative Teaching Press

Minute 71

Name _____

1. 50 − 10 = _____

2. 42 + 40 = _____

3. Mei wants to buy a fruit roll for 12¢. She has one dime in her pocket. How much more does she need to buy the fruit roll? _____ ¢

4. Do 2 feet equal 24 inches?   Circle: Yes   or   No

For questions 5 and 6, write the number of parts.
Circle: equal   or   not equal

5.    _____ parts   equal   not equal

6.   _____ parts   equal   not equal

7. 5 + 5 + 5 = _____   ⬚ + ⬚ + ⬚

8. 84
   − 45

9. Write the number five hundred forty-six. _____

10. Write how much money in all. _____ ¢

Second-Grade Math Minutes © 2002 Creative Teaching Press

Minute 72

Name _____

1.
```
  90
- 66
```

2.
```
  364
+ 138
```

3.
```
   37
   41
+ 15
```

4. Write the numbers that come before and after.

_____ 401 _____

5. 6 + 6 + 6 = _____

☆☆☆
☆☆☆
+
☆☆☆
☆☆☆
+
☆☆☆
☆☆☆

For questions 6 and 7, write the number of equal parts that are shaded.

6. ⬕ ▢ ⎯ 2   shaded part
equal parts

7. ▦ ▢ ⎯ 3   shaded parts
equal parts

8. Jenna has 3 books. Nate has 9 books. Hannah has 6 books. How many books do they have altogether? _____ books

9. Write how many hours have passed. _____ hours

10. Use < or >.   430 _____ 420

Second-Grade Math Minutes © 2002 Creative Teaching Press

Minute 73

Name _____

1. 54 – 10 = _____

2. Circle the cone:

3. 66
    + 38

4. 38
    + 10

5. How much does the melon weigh? _____ pounds

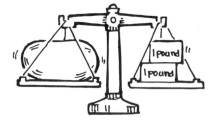

6. Find the pattern. Write the missing number.
875, 880, 885, _____, 895

7. Write how much money in all. _____ ¢

8. Write the number eight hundred seventy-one. _____

9. Write the numbers that come before and after. _____ 350 _____

10. Tyler ate 12 grapes. Alfredo ate 8 grapes. How many more grapes did Tyler eat than Alfredo? _____ grapes

Second-Grade Math Minutes © 2002 Creative Teaching Press

Minute 74

Name _____

1. Write the missing numbers. _____, 300, 400, _____, 600

2. 75 – 10 = _____

3. Circle how much a pencil might cost: 25¢ $25

4. Circle the rectangular prism:

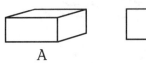

A B C

5. Use < or >. 518 _____ 531

6. 272
      – 129

7. 87¢
      – 30¢

For questions 8 and 9, write the number of equal parts that are shaded.

8. ⬜ / 3 shaded parts
          equal parts

9. ⬜ / 4 shaded parts
          equal parts

10. There are 16 ounces in 1 pound. Circle: True or False

Second-Grade Math Minutes © 2002 Creative Teaching Press

Minute 75

Name _____

1. Write 10 more than 100. _____

2. Write the number eight hundred seven. _____

3. Mike has 3 rocks. Jan has 10 rocks. How many rocks do they have altogether? _____ rocks

4. Write the time. _____

5. Circle the pyramid:

     A   B   C

6. 23 − 10 = _____

7. In the number 280, which digit is in the tens place? _____

In questions 8 and 9, does each hold more or less than 1 pint? Circle the answer.

   2 cups = 1 pint

8.   more   less

9.   more   less

10. Use < or >.   757 _____ 577

Second-Grade Math Minutes © 2002 Creative Teaching Press

Minute 76

Name _____

1. Circle the name of the shape:
   triangle   circle   rectangle

2. Write 10 more than 220. _____

3. Add. Write the amount.    + 20¢ = ____¢

4. Circle the shape with no corners: □ △ ◯
   A   B   C

5. Write the distance around the shape. _____

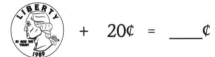

6. Write how many parts are shaded.

   $\dfrac{}{4}$

7. 88
   + 6

Use the pictograph to complete questions 8–10.

Fish Caught

🐟 = 1 fish

8. How many fish did the yellow boat catch? _____ fish

9. How many fish did the red boat catch? _____ fish

10. Which boat caught the fewest fish? _____

Second-Grade Math Minutes © 2002 Creative Teaching Press

Minute 77

Name _____

1. Write the number that comes between.   609 _____ 611

2. Write the amount.   = _____ ¢

In questions 3 and 4, which holds more or less than 1 quart? Circle the answer.

   4 cups = 1 quart

3.   more   less

4.   more   less

5. Use < or >.   598 _____ 589   **6.**   507
                                            + 276

7. Write what part is shaded.

8. 3 + 3 + 3 + 3 + 3 = _____

9. Circle the digit in the hundreds place: 563

10.   27
        + 53

Second-Grade Math Minutes © 2002 Creative Teaching Press

Minute 78

Name _____

1. 85
       − 10

2. 894
       − 119

3. 18
       + 53

4. Write one hundred twenty-one. _____

5. Add. Write the amount.  + 10¢ = _____ ¢

6. Use < or >.   876 _____ 786

For questions 7 and 8, circle if each holds more or less than 1 gallon.

 1 gallon = 4 quarts

7. a bathtub filled with water   more   less

8. a cup of hot chocolate   more   less

9. 35 + 10 = _____

10. Max has 5 plates. Each plate holds 5 gumballs.
How many gumballs does Max have in all? _____ gumballs

Second-Grade Math Minutes © 2002 Creative Teaching Press

Minute 79

Name _____

Use the picture to complete questions 1 and 2.

1. Draw 2 balls in each box.

2. How many balls in all? _____ balls

3. Write how many parts are shaded.

$$\frac{}{5}$$

For questions 4 and 5, circle if each holds more or less than 1 liter.

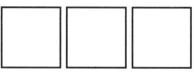 = 1 liter

4. a swimming pool   more   less

5. a soup spoon   more   less

6. Is the area of the shape 6 squares?
Circle: Yes   or   No

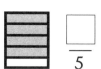

7. 75 – 10 = _____

8. Does this equal $3.51?
Circle: Yes   or   No

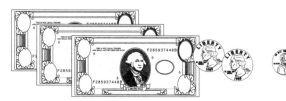

9. Use <, >, or =.   Seven _____ 7

10. 48 + 10 = _____

Second-Grade Math Minutes © 2002 Creative Teaching Press

Minute 80

Name _____

1. Write the perimeter of the shape.
   _____ centimeters

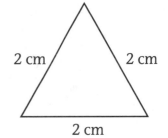

2 cm / 2 cm

2 cm

2. 93
   − 54

3. Circle the name of the solid:
   sphere   cone   cylinder

4. Do the carrots weigh more or less
   than 1 pound?   Circle the answer.

more   less

5. 84 + 10 = _____

6. Write how many squares cover the shape.
   The area of the shape is _____ squares.

7. 739
   − 476

8. A square has _____ sides and _____ corners.

9. Write the number two hundred eighty-nine. _____

10. Does this money equal $5.10?   Circle: Yes   or   No

Second-Grade Math Minutes © 2002 Creative Teaching Press

Minute 81

Name _____

1. 16¢
    + 24¢

2. Write the time. _____

3. Is this a line of symmetry?
Circle: Yes or No

4. Write the number five hundred three.
_____

5. 98
    − 10

6. What fraction of the rectangle is shaded? Circle the answer.

$\frac{2}{6}$ $\frac{3}{6}$ $\frac{4}{6}$

7. 79 + 10 = _____

Use the pictograph to complete questions 8–10.

8. How many children like
to go to the zoo?
_____ children

9. Do more children like
the park or the zoo?
_____

10. How many children like the aquarium? _____ children

Favorite Field Trip

Zoo	🚌 🚌 🚌
Park	🚌 🚌 🚐
Aquarium	🚌 🚌 🚌 🚌 🚐

🚌 = 2 children

Second-Grade Math Minutes © 2002 Creative Teaching Press

Minute 82

Name _____

1. Circle the fraction that names the shaded part:

$\frac{2}{5}$ $\frac{3}{5}$ $\frac{4}{5}$

2. Tricia swam for 2 hours. Write what time she stopped.

Start Time End Time _____

3. Color one box for the vegetable each child likes.
4 children like peas.   5 children like carrots.

Favorite Vegetables

Peas					
Carrots					

4.   14
    + 78

5. A swimming pool holds more than 1 liter of water.
Circle: True or False

6. A rectangle has _____ corners and _____ sides.

7. 63 – 10 = _____

8. 247 = _____ hundreds _____ tens _____ ones

9. 6 + 6 + 6 = _____

10. A cup holds more than 1 gallon. Circle: True or False

Second-Grade Math Minutes © 2002 Creative Teaching Press

Minute 83

Name _____

1.
$$\begin{array}{r} 51 \\ -\ 47 \\ \hline \end{array}$$

2. Write the number six hundred two. _____

3. A trash can holds more than 1 liter.   Circle: True   or   False

For questions 4 and 5, find the pattern. Write what comes next.

4. $0.33 $0.34 $0.35   _____

5. $1.24 $2.24 $3.24   _____

6. 406 = _____ hundreds   _____ tens   _____ ones

7. Write the name of the solid.
_____

8. 33 + 10 = _____

9.
$$\begin{array}{r} 590 \\ -\ 274 \\ \hline \end{array}$$

10. Write the fraction that names the shaded part.

$\dfrac{}{4}$

Second-Grade Math Minutes © 2002 Creative Teaching Press

Minute 84

Name _____

1. There are 4 quarts in 1 gallon.   Circle: True   or   False

For questions 2 and 3, add and multiply to find how many there are in all.

2. 2 + 2 + 2 + 2 = _____   4 x 2 = _____   ☆ ☆ ☆ ☆
                                                        ☆ ☆ ☆ ☆

3. 3 + 3 = _____   2 x 3 = _____   ● ● ●   ● ● ●

4. Write the fraction that names the shaded part.

$\dfrac{\square}{5}$

5. Which weighs more? Underline the answer.
an apple   a watermelon

6. 6 + 3 + 5 = _____

7. Write how many squares cover the shape.
The area of the shape is _____ squares.

8. Use <, >, or =.   thirty-nine _____ 37

9. Write the time. _____

10. Write the amount.

+ 53¢ = $_____

Second-Grade Math Minutes © 2002 Creative Teaching Press

Minute 85

Name _____

1. 8 quarts are less than 1 gallon   Circle: True   or   False

For questions 2 and 3, add and multiply to find how many there are in all.

2. 5 + 5 + 5 = _____   3 x 5 = _____

3. 3 + 3 + 3 = _____   3 x 3 = _____

4. 45 − 10 = _____

5. Write how many equal parts there are.

For questions 6 and 7, circle if each weighs more or less than 1 kilogram.

6. a chair   more   less

7. a banana   more   less   weighs about 1 kilogram

8. $3.85   **9.**   110 + 10 = _____
     − 1.34

10. Circle what you would use to measure the length of your arm:
          inches   feet   pounds

Second-Grade Math Minutes © 2002 Creative Teaching Press

Minute 86

Name _____

1. Write what fraction is shaded.

$\frac{\square}{8}$

2. $85 - 10 =$ _____

3. Circle what you will see if you trace the shape:

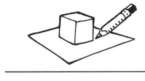

    A   B   C

4. $75 + 10 =$ _____

Use the bar graph to complete questions 5–7.

5. Which snack is the most favorite?
_____

6. How many more children chose pretzels than fruit? _____ more children

7. What is the least favorite snack? _____

Children's Favorite Snack

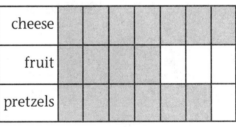

8. Circle the shape that shows a line of symmetry:

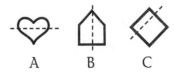

    A   B   C

9. Use < or >.   856 _____ 956

10. Write the number six hundred eleven. _____

Second-Grade Math Minutes © 2002 Creative Teaching Press

Minute 87

Name _____

1. Use >, <, or =.   25¢ _____ 10¢ + 10¢

2. Write 1 less and 1 more.   _____ 635 _____

3. 849 = _____ hundreds _____ tens _____ ones

4. $3.94
   − 1.33
   ‾‾‾‾‾‾

5. Write what comes next.   947, 948, 949, _____

6. The area of the shape is _____ squares.

7. Write three hundred five. _____

8. 85 + 10 = _____

9. Tristan has 182 baseball cards. Camille has 128 baseball cards. Who has the most baseball cards? _____

10. How many months are in 1 year? _____ months

Second-Grade Math Minutes © 2002 Creative Teaching Press

Minute 88

Name _____

1. Write the number one hundred twenty-five. _____

2. Use <, >, or =.   2 dimes _____ 20¢

Use the table to complete questions 3 and 4.

Katie's Chores

Job	Start Time	Amount of Time Job Took
Put away toys	8:30	10 minutes
Make bed	9:15	15 minutes

3. What time did Katie finish putting away her toys? _____

4. What time did Katie finish making her bed? _____

5. Write the fraction.

    ⬚ shaded parts
                        ⬚ equal parts

6. Use <, >, or =.

   Eighty-seven _____ 78

7.   18¢
    + 25¢
    ‾‾‾‾‾

8. Write 100 less. _____ 250

9. 11 + 20 = _____

10. Write how many hours have passed.
    _____ hours

Second-Grade Math Minutes © 2002 Creative Teaching Press

Minute 89

Name _____

1. There are 8 days in 1 week.   Circle: True   or   False

2. Write the time. _____

3. Write the fraction.

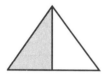   ☐ shaded parts
                        ☐ equal parts

4.   43¢
        − 15¢

5. The area of the shape is _____ squares.

For questions 6 and 7, add and multiply to find how many there are in all.

6. 5 + 5 = _____   2 x 5 = _____

7. 4 + 4 + 4 = _____   3 x 4 = _____

8. Read the thermometer.
Circle how many degrees: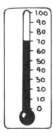

60°F   70°F   80°F

9. A balloon is lighter than 1 kilogram.
Circle: True   or   False

10.   353
         − 128

Second-Grade Math Minutes © 2002 Creative Teaching Press

Minute 90

Name _____

1. The perimeter of the shape is _____ .

2. Write the fraction.

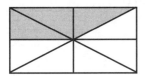

☐ shaded parts

☐ equal parts

3. Add and multiply.

$4 + 4 + 4 + 4 =$ _____

$4 \times 4 =$ _____

4. 239
   − 45

5. Write the number nine hundred thirty-three.

   _____

6. Write 100 less and 100 more.   _____ 896 _____

7. Write how many hours have passed.
   _____ hours

8. Circle how many degrees:
   30°F   40°F   50°F

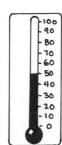

9. 124
   + 47

10. $3.87
    − .72

Second-Grade Math Minutes © 2002 Creative Teaching Press

Minute 91

Name _____

1. Is this a line of symmetry?
   Circle: Yes   or   No

2. Write the number nine hundred sixty-four. _____

3.   256
    − 73

4. $1.25
    + 1.50

5. The area of the shape is _____ squares.

6. A rectangle has _____ corners and _____ sides.

7. Add and multiply.

   ☆ ☆   2 + 2 = _____
   ☆ ☆   2 x 2 = _____

8. The first month of the year is _____ .

9.   342
    + 38

10. Write the fraction.

   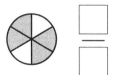

Second-Grade Math Minutes © 2002 Creative Teaching Press

Minute 92

Name _____

1. Write the fraction.

2. A bathtub holds more than 1 liter of water.
Circle: True or False

3.   265
  − 85

4.   150 + 10 = _____

5. Write how many degrees. _____°F
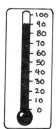

Use the pictograph to complete questions 6–8.

6. How many people traveled
by car? _____ people

7. Did more people choose
the plane or car?
_____

8. How many more people chose the
bus than chose the train? _____ more people

Trip Transportation

car	🧍 🧍 🧍 🧍 🧍
train	🧍 🧍
plane	🧍 🧍 🧍 🧍 🧍 🧍
bus	🧍 🧍 🧍 🧍

🧍 = 2 people

9. A feather is lighter than 1 kilogram.
Circle: True   or   False

10.   328
  + 134

Second-Grade Math Minutes © 2002 Creative Teaching Press

Minute 93

Name _____

1. Write 100 less and 100 more. _____ 120 _____

2. 505
   + 15

3. 808 = _____ hundreds _____ tens _____ ones

4. Use <, >, or =.   1 half-dollar _____ 62¢

5. Do you think a pencil might cost 25¢ or $25? _____

6. Write the fraction.   **7.**   453
                                       – 108

8. If you drop a glass bottle, will it break? Underline the answer.

sure to happen / impossible

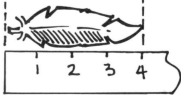

9. About how long is the feather?
_____ centimeters

10. Add and multiply.

3 + 3 = _____
2 x 3 = _____

Second-Grade Math Minutes © 2002 Creative Teaching Press

Minute 94

Name _____

1. Multiply.

$2 \times 3 =$ _____

$3 \times 2 =$ _____

For questions 2 and 3, circle if each weighs more or less than 1 pound.

weighs about 1 pound

2. a watermelon   more   less

3. a carrot   more   less

4. $95 - 10 =$ _____

Use the graph to complete questions 5–7.

5. Go across 2. Go up 1. Do you find an elephant or a bear?

_____

6. Go across 4. Go up 3. Do you find a giraffe or a lion?

_____

7. Where is the snake?
Go across _____. Go up _____.

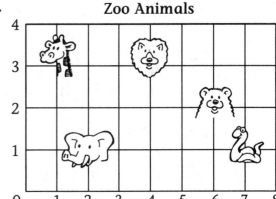

Zoo Animals

8. $4.50
    − .18

9. $58 + 10 =$ _____

10. A triangle has _____ sides and _____ corners.

Second-Grade Math Minutes © 2002 Creative Teaching Press

Minute 95

Name _____

1. Multiply.

$2 \times 4 =$ _____

$4 \times 2 =$ _____

2. 926
  − 572
  _____

3. Write the fraction.

4. 223 = _____ hundreds _____ tens _____ ones

5. Bob has $4.35. He wants to buy a book that costs $4.28. Does he have enough money?   Circle: Yes   or   No

6. Write 100 less and 100 more.   _____ 400 _____

7. The area of the shape is _____ squares.

8. A puppy weighs about _____ pounds.   Circle: 10   or   100

9. Use <, >, or =.   253 _____ 235

10. 5 pennies equal 1 nickel.   Circle: True   or   False

Second-Grade Math Minutes © 2002 Creative Teaching Press

Minute 96

Name _____

1. Write the number two hundred thirty-one. _____

2. Write the perimeter. _____

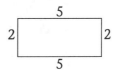

3. 89 + 10 = _____

Use the pictograph to complete questions 4–6.

Children's Favorite Sport

Skating		☺ ☺ ☺ ☺
Basketball		☺ ☺
Soccer		☺ ☺ ☺ ☺ ☺

☺ = 5 children

4. How many children like soccer? _____ children

5. Is skating liked more than soccer? _____

6. How many more children like soccer than basketball? _____ more children

7. Where is the star on the graph?
_____ across _____ up

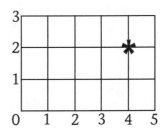

8. 454
    − 58

9. A paper cup holds more than 1 gallon. Circle: True or False

10. Use <, >, or =.

_____ $5.00

Second-Grade Math Minutes © 2002 Creative Teaching Press

Minute 97

Name _____

1. Write 10 less and 10 more. _____ 245 _____

2. 930
      − 92

3. Write the time. _____

4. There are 12 cherries.
Write how many groups of 4 there are.

_____ groups of 4

5. Circle one half: $\frac{1}{2}$ $\frac{1}{3}$ $\frac{1}{4}$

6. An aquarium holds more than 1 quart.
Circle: True   or   False

7. Sally has $5.32. She wants to buy lunch for $5.23.
Does she have enough money? _____

8. Multiply.

$2 \times 5 =$ _____
$5 \times 2 =$ _____

9. 234
      + 47

10. Write the perimeter. _____

Second-Grade Math Minutes © 2002 Creative Teaching Press

Minute 98

Name _____

1. 649 = _____ hundreds _____ tens _____ ones

2. 243
   + 162

3. $1.66
   + 2.52

4. Circle one third: $\frac{1}{2}$ $\frac{1}{3}$ $\frac{1}{4}$

5. Find the pattern. Write what comes next.

   $4.12 $5.12 $6.12   _____

6. Write the number one hundred eleven. _____

7. Maria started her homework at 3:00. It took her 45 minutes to do it. What time did she finish? _____

8. Find the perimeter. _____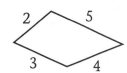

9. 95 – 10 = _____

10. How much is 400 + 30 + 3?   Circle the answer.

    343   334   433

Second-Grade Math Minutes © 2002 Creative Teaching Press

Minute 99

Name _____

1. 98 – 10 = _____

2. How much is 300 + 20 + 9?   239   329   392
   Circle the answer.

3. Multiply.
    3 x 5 = _____
   5 x 3 = _____

4. Write the fraction.

5. Write how many groups of 5 are in 10.
   _____ groups of 5

6.   616
   – 62

7. Write the number seven hundred sixty-three. _____

8. Use <, >, or =. $6.36 _____ $7.36

9. 1 gallon equals _____ quarts

10. 87 + 10 = _____

Second-Grade Math Minutes © 2002 Creative Teaching Press

Minute 100

Name _____

1. Write 10 less. _____ 549

2. How many cups equal 1 pint? _____ cups

3. Write the perimeter. _____

(square with 4 on each side)

4. 120 + 10 = _____

5. The area of the shape is _____ squares.

Use the pictograph to complete questions 6–8.

Kinds of Fish at the Store

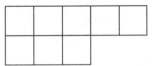

goldfish	🐟 🐟 🐟 🐟 🐟 🐟
angelfish	🐟 🐟 🐟 🐟
tiger fish	🐟 🐟 🐟

🐟 = 5 fish

6. How many goldfish are there? _____ goldfish

7. Are there more angelfish or tiger fish? _____

8. How many more goldfish are there than tiger fish? _____ more goldfish

9. 405
     − 121

10. Write the degrees. _____ °F

Second-Grade Math Minutes © 2002 Creative Teaching Press

Minute Answer Key

Minute 1
1. 4
2. 6
3. 4
4. 8
5. 7
6. >
7. 8
8. 3
9. square
10. triangle

Minute 2
1. <
2. >
3. 2
4. 5
5. 9
6. 2
7. 7
8. 17
9. 9
10. 5

Minute 3
1. 8, 10
2. 2
3. 7
4. 9
5. 7
6. 6
7. >
8. 6
9. strawberry
10. chocolate

Minute 4
1. 2
2. 7
3. <
4. 16
5. blue
6. 5
7. 50
8. 34, 38
9. circle
10. triangle

Minute 5
1. 8
2. 5
3. 11
4. 3
5. 24
6. 6
7. 3
8. dime
9. penny
10. quarter

Minute 6
1. 1¢
2. 25¢
3. 10¢
4. 55, 58
5. 63
6. 7
7. 46
8. 12¢
9. 10¢
10. 29¢

Minute 7
1. >
2. <
3. <
4. True
5. 8
6. 12
7. 8
8. 15
9. 18
10. 3

Minute 8
1. 5, 6
2. 32
3. 7
4. 20, 30
5. 9¢
6. 25¢
7. 12¢
8. 13
9. <
10. 2

Minute 9
1. 9
2. 5
3. False
4. snake
5. True
6. 15
7. 14
8. 35
9. 50
10. ◯

Minute 10
1. 13
2. 14
3. triangle
4. 53¢
5. 8
6. 38
7. 22
8. 5
9. 15
10. ▢

Minute 11
1. 9:00
2. 11:00
3. 18
4. <
5. more
6. 15¢
7. Yes
8. △
9. 13
10. 15

Minute 12
1. 45
2. 5
3. 3:00
4. 6:00
5. 72
6. 43
7. 29
8. >
9. 9
10. 18

Minute 13
1. 15
2. Student draws 10:00.
3. 26
4. 10
5. 22
6. 45
7. car
8. fifth
9. bicycle
10. 39¢

Minute 14
1. 37¢
2. 43¢
3. 36
4. 9
5. 10
6. 4
7. 8
8. 5
9. frogs
10. 10

Minute 15
1. 27
2. 9
3. 13
4. 17
5. 40
6. 3:30
7. 7:30
8. 3, 6
9. 5, 2
10. 4, 9

Minute 16
1. oval
2. rectangle
3. triangle
4. 74
5. 4
6. blue
7. 10
8. 11
9. 68
10. ▭

Minute 17
1. 13
2. 66¢
3. 48¢
4. 12
5. 43
6. 4, 9
7. 9, 4
8. 17
9. 51
10. True

Minute 18
1. 79
2. 45
3. 18
4. 5:30
5. 8:30
6. 56
7. 2
8. 76
9. 53
10. square

Minute 19
1. 8
2. False
3. 12
4. 45
5. 12
6. 53
7. 74
8. 70
9. 42
10. rectangle

Minute 20
1. 17
2. 9
3. 10
4. 9 ones
5. 2 tens
6. 89
7. 62¢
8. 73
9. >
10. <

Second-Grade Math Minutes © 2002 Creative Teaching Press

Minute Answer Key

Minute 21
1. 3 + 3 = 6
2. 5 + 5 = 10
3. 7
4. D
5. B
6. F
7. 1 dime, 1 nickel, 3 pennies
8. 2 dimes
9. 28
10. Student draws 2:00.

Minute 22
1. ⬭
2. 33
3. nickel
4. quarter
5. 19
6. 9
7. 27
8. 4 + 4 = 8
9. 6 + 6 = 12
10. △

Minute 23
1. 79
2. 4
3. 8
4. 46
5. 5:30
6. 11
7. 2
8. 8
9. 72
10. 99

Minute 24
1. 18
2. 16
3. 35
4. Student draws 12:30.
5. 68
6. 20
7. 75
8. 14
9. 7, 9
10. 68¢

Minute 25
1. False
2. 13
3. 81
4. 12
5. diamond
6. 8
7. 1:00
8. 17
9. 49
10. 20

Minute 26
1. 9
2. 3
3. 33
4. 50
5. Mary
6. Katie
7. 2
8. 35
9. 8
10. 21

Minute 27
1. 2:30
2. 68
3. Student draws 9:00.
4. 25
5. 57
6. 3
7. 6 + 9 = 15
8. 10 + 4 = 14
9. quarter
10. 6

Minute 28
1. 66
2. 82
3. 96
4. 9
5. 3:15
6. 9
7. True
8. 1:30
9. 3:30
10. 5

Minute 29
1. 4:15
2. 33
3. 6
4. 8
5. 12
6. 18
7. >
8. <
9. 8
10. 50

Minute 30
1. January
2. 16
3. 3
4. 6:15
5. first, second, third
6. fourth, fifth, sixth
7. 98
8. 33
9. 85
10. Student circles rectangle.

Minute 31
1. Student draws 3:15.
2. 11
3. brown eyes
4. 24
5. 4
6. 27¢
7. 18
8. 45
9. 11
10. October, November, December

Minute 32
1. 30
2. 78
3. 8
4. 3
5. 3:25
6. True
7. 34
8. 20
9. 39
10. December

Minute 33
1. April
2. 22
3. 4:45
4. 6:30
5. –
6. 94
7. 25
8. 8, 9
9. 25¢
10. 12

Minute 34
1. 14
2. 15
3. False
4. sisters
5. 3
6. 20
7. 9:55
8. 6
9. 8
10. 88

Minute 35
1. 1:45
2. 48
3. 45
4. +
5. 13
6. 3
7. 7, 8
8. 17
9. 48
10. 78

Minute 36
1. 74
2. 2
3. 85¢
4. triangle
5. rectangle
6. 8:15
7. 46
8. –
9. 49
10. 9

Minute 37
1. Thursday
2. Saturday
3. Tuesday
4. 95
5. 24
6. 5
7. 53
8. 5
9. 30
10. 1st

Minute 38
1. True
2. C
3. +
4. 47¢
5. 37¢
6. 6
7. 1
8. 52
9. 4, 8
10. 99

Minute 39
1. 104
2. 91
3. =
4. 9
5. False
6. 4:35
7. 96
8. 37
9. 7
10. fishing, biking

Minute 40
1. 3
2. hexagon
3. 4
4. 35¢
5. 75
6. 168
7. Yes
8. 39
9. 88
10. 149

Second-Grade Math Minutes © 2002 Creative Teaching Press

Minute Answer Key

Minute 41
1. 83
2. 4
3. 4
4. 3
5. 15
6. Student draws 3:00.
7. 50
8. 130
9. 3
10. 58

Minute 42
1. pentagon
2. 151
3. 15
4. 29
5. 1:40
6. 88
7. 2
8. 8
9. 5
10. 7

Minute 43
1. rectangle
2. 79
3. 3
4. 53
5. <
6. 851
7. 36
8. B
9. C
10. 65¢

Minute 44
1. 174
2. 100
3. 41
4. 1
5. 151
6. Student draws 5:55.
7. feet
8. inches
9. 10
10. 5

Minute 45
1. 54
2. 200
3. 630
4. 9
5. 6
6. 3
7. 18
8. 9:00
9. 37¢
10. Amy

Minute 46
1. 518
2. –
3. False
4. 3
5. 358
6. 2:30
7. 20
8. 1 quarter, 1 dime, 1 nickel, 2 pennies
9. 1 quarter, 1 dime, 3 pennies
10. 137, 141, 142

Minute 47
1. 25¢
2. 22
3. 3:15
4. 4, 5, 8
5. 56
6. 67, 75
7. 96
8. 7
9. 9
10. 12

Minute 48
1. 132
2. May
3. Yes
4. Yes
5. 6:30
6. 10
7. 51¢
8. Sharon
9. 22
10. circle

Minute 49
1. 978
2. 151, 153, 154
3. 13
4. 17
5. pizza
6. 57¢
7. 74
8. D
9. I
10. G

Minute 50
1. 45
2. 56
3. 10
4. 719
5. 4:50
6. 7:40
7. 186, 189
8. 629
9. False
10. feet

Minute 51
1. 2
2. 15
3. 52
4. 7
5. 10
6. 92, 98
7. 3
8. 10
9. 30
10. 10

Minute 52
1. 22
2. 20
3. 113
4. 400
5. 2
6. 735
7. 2
8. True
9. 10 hours
10. True

Minute 53
1. 217
2. 99
3. 461
4. C
5. 500
6. 10
7. cube
8. cylinder
9. 4
10. No

Minute 54
1. cone
2. 3
3. 54
4. 600, 900
5. A
6. C
7. 20
8. B
9. 129
10. 100

Minute 55
1. Yes
2. 12
3. 154
4. 9:30
5. 400, 700
6. 60¢
7. 874
8. A
9. False
10. 509

Minute 56
1. 659
2. Yes
3. 966
4. False
5. 130, 134
6. 983
7. True
8. 85
9. rectangular prism
10. cone

Minute 57
1. No
2. feet
3. feet
4. 10:45
5. 337
6. 515
7. 200, 400
8. 115
9. 91
10. 525

Minute 58
1. True
2.
3. 337
4. 83
5. 11
6. 9
7. 515
8. 51
9. 356
10. 70¢

Minute 59
1. 218
2. 26
3. 2, 4, 8
4. 781
5. >
6. 32
7. 712
8. centimeters
9. meters
10. 5:30

Minute 60
1. B
2. 329
3. 431
4. 45
5. cube
6. 43¢
7. 790
8. 600, 900
9. 11:55
10. 981

Second-Grade Math Minutes © 2002 Creative Teaching Press

Minute Answer Key

Minute 61
1. 103
2. cone
3. meters
4. centimeters
5. 5, 6, 3
6. 53
7. 101
8. 9
9. 199
10. $1.00

Minute 62
1. 5:00
2. 413
3. meters
4. Student draws x over circle.
5. 5
6. –
7. Friday
8. 77¢
9. 12
10. 6, 9, 7

Minute 63
1. 788, 790
2. 55
3. 12
4. 40
5. Monday, Friday
6. Wednesday
7. 6, 3, 2
8. 8
9. B
10. Sunday

Minute 64
1. 4, 2, 0
2. 307
3. 1 quater
4. 2 dimes and 1 nickel
5. 790
6. 91
7. 56
8. 135
9. 12
10. 2:25

Minute 65
1. 395
2. 90
3. 9¢
4. 40¢
5. 12
6. >
7. 12
8. B
9. 438
10. 7

Minute 66
1. 8
2. 1,115
3. 5
4. 58
5. Yes
6. cylinder
7. 93
8. 29¢
9. e
10. a

Minute 67
1. 6
2. 109
3. 1,059
4. rectangular prism
5. >
6. 15
7. $1.16
8. 455
9. not happen
10. will happen

Minute 68
1. $2.33
2. 99
3. 2
4. 96
5. <
6. square
7. 9
8. Tall Tales
9. Yes
10. 6

Minute 69
1. 105
2. 753
3. 86
4. Yes
5. 317
6. No
7. not happen
8. will happen
9. True
10. 6

Minute 70
1. 9
2. 298
3.
4. 16
5. 7:25
6. No
7. 3
8. 6
9. 29
10. <

Minute 71
1. 40
2. 82
3. 2¢
4. Yes
5. 3, equal
6. 4, not equal
7. 15
8. 39
9. 546
10. 72¢

Minute 72
1. 24
2. 502
3. 93
4. 400, 402
5. 18
6. 1
7. 2
8. 18
9. 3
10. >

Minute 73
1. 44
2.
3. 104
4. 48
5. 2
6. 890
7. 61¢
8. 871
9. 349, 351
10. 4

Minute 74
1. 200, 500
2. 65
3. 25¢
4. A
5. <
6. 143
7. 57¢
8. 2
9. 2
10. True

Minute 75
1. 110
2. 807
3. 13
4. 4:15
5. C
6. 13
7. 8
8. less
9. more
10. >

Minute 76
1. triangle
2. 230
3. 45¢
4. C
5. 7
6. 3
7. 94
8. 7
9. 5
10. blue boat

Minute 77
1. 610
2. 39¢
3. more
4. less
5. >
6. 783
7. 1
8. 15
9. 5
10. 80

Minute 78
1. 75
2. 775
3. 71
4. 121
5. 66¢
6. >
7. more
8. less
9. 45
10. 25

Minute 79
1. Student draws 2 balls in each box.
2. 6
3. 4
4. more
5. less
6. Yes
7. 65
8. Yes
9. =
10. 58

Minute 80
1. 6
2. 39
3. cylinder
4. less
5. 94
6. 4
7. 263
8. 4, 4
9. 289
10. No

Second-Grade Math Minutes © 2002 Creative Teaching Press

Minute Answer Key

Minute 81
1. 40¢
2. 11:40
3. No
4. 503
5. 88
6. $^4/_6$
7. 89
8. 6
9. zoo
10. 9

Minute 82
1. $^3/_5$
2. 3:30
3. Student colors graph.
4. 92
5. True
6. 4, 4
7. 53
8. 2, 4, 7
9. 18
10. False

Minute 83
1. 4
2. 602
3. True
4. $0.36
5. $4.24
6. 4, 0, 6
7. cube
8. 43
9. 316
10. 3

Minute 84
1. True
2. 8, 8
3. 6, 6
4. 2
5. a watermelon
6. 14
7. 8
8. >
9. 6:55
10. $3.53

Minute 85
1. False
2. 15, 15
3. 9, 9
4. 35
5. 5
6. more
7. less
8. $2.51
9. 120
10. inches

Minute 86
1. 5
2. 75
3. B
4. 85
5. cheese
6. 2
7. fruit
8. B
9. <
10. 611

Minute 87
1. >
2. 625, 645
3. 8, 4, 9
4. $2.61
5. 950
6. 9
7. 305
8. 95
9. Tristan
10. 12

Minute 88
1. 125
2. =
3. 8:40
4. 9:30
5. $^3/_6$
6. >
7. 43¢
8. 150
9. 31
10. 7

Minute 89
1. False
2. 12:05
3. $^1/_2$
4. 28¢
5. 8
6. 10, 10
7. 12, 12
8. 70°F
9. True
10. 225

Minute 90
1. 9
2. $^3/_8$
3. 16, 16
4. 194
5. 933
6. 796, 996
7. 4
8. 50°F
9. 171
10. $3.15

Minute 91
1. No
2. 964
3. 183
4. $2.75
5. 10
6. 4, 4
7. 4, 4
8. January
9. 380
10. $^4/_6$ or $^2/_3$

Minute 92
1. $^2/_4$ or $^1/_2$
2. True
3. 180
4. 160
5. 90°F
6. 10
7. plane
8. 4
9. True
10. 462

Minute 93
1. 20, 220
2. 520
3. 8, 0, 8
4. <
5. 25¢
6. $^2/_3$
7. 345
8. sure to happen
9. 4
10. 6, 6

Minute 94
1. 6, 6
2. more
3. less
4. 85
5. elephant
6. lion
7. 7, 1
8. $4.32
9. 68
10. 3, 3

Minute 95
1. 8, 8
2. 354
3. $^2/_5$
4. 2, 2, 3
5. Yes
6. 300, 500
7. 9
8. 10
9. >
10. True

Minute 96
1. 231
2. 14
3. 99
4. 25
5. No
6. 15
7. 4, 2
8. 396
9. False
10. =

Minute 97
1. 235, 255
2. 838
3. 5:55
4. 3
5. $^1/_2$
6. True
7. Yes
8. 10, 10
9. 281
10. 13

Minute 98
1. 6, 4, 9
2. 405
3. $4.18
4. $^1/_3$
5. $7.12
6. 111
7. 3:45
8. 14
9. 85
10. 433

Minute 99
1. 88
2. 329
3. 15, 15
4. $^2/_3$
5. 2
6. 554
7. 763
8. <
9. 4
10. 97

Minute 100
1. 539
2. 2
3. 16
4. 130
5. 8
6. 30
7. angelfish
8. 15
9. 284
10. 30°F

Second-Grade Math Minutes © 2002 Creative Teaching Press